THIS BOOK IS DEDICATED TO MY CHILDREN
TAYLOR, CHANDLER, AND KEETON, WHO MAKE
ME PROUD EVERY DAY AND WHO I LOVE ALMOST
AS MUCH AS THESE PUPPIES... JUST KIDDING. WHO
CAN COMPETE WITH PUPPIES? AND TO MY SWEET
GRAMMY, WHO LOVED TO READ TO ME AS A CHILD.
YOU ARE MISSED DEARLY.

The Silver Dozen

LABRADOR RETRIEVERS

EST. 2016

DALLAS, TEXAS

Cover art by Anya studenc Caruso
Professional Photography by Molly Coulter
Design and layout by Marquett Brewster

ISBN: 978-0-9600315-0-4
Library of Congress Control Number: 2018967231

First Printing Edition 2018
Published by Marquis Crowne

THE Silver DOZEN

WRITTEN BY MARQUETT BREWSTER

ILLUSTRATED BY ANYA STUDENC CARUSO

Marquis Crowne

It was a sunny, Sunday afternoon much like any other in late February. Except for on this day, the most wonderful thing happened...

Twelve tiny, furry, squeaky, silver puppies were born. There were seven boys and five girls. And even though they all looked the same, they all were different and special...

just like you!

Mama Bella was so proud of them all.
She fed them, played with them, and
loved on them everyday…
all day, for weeks.

Those twelve tiny, blue-eyed,
furry, squeaky, silver puppies,
kept her very, very busy. They took
naps because they got
very, very tired.

Do YOU ever take naps?

As each week went by, they grew bigger and bigger. Like any proud mama, she wanted to take their picture. All twelve of the puppies - there was Cooper, Sterling, Chance, Clementine, Blue, Lincoln, Isabelle, Churchill, Aspen, Clancy, Gator, and Amigo, all lined up on the back of the couch.

They wiggled their little bodies and wagged their silver tails. Molly, the photographer, told them to look at her and say "treats". So they did…well except the two near the one end. Chance couldn't leave his sister Sterling's ear alone. He was being so silly.

Do YOU ever act silly?

They weren't the only puppies
that acted up. When they were outside,
the puppies all loved to chase Dolly,
their sister-chicken. Churchill was the
worst of them about running after her,
feathers flying, wings flapping, and
her head bobbing in his mouth until
mama called him out.

"Churchill!!! We don't eat the chicken! She is family too."

Dolly might have lost a feather,
or two, or three, but she secretly liked
to play with Churchill.
They were friends.
He was her best friend.

Do YOU have a friend that you like
to play with?

These tiny, furry, squeaky, silver puppies were getting so much bigger and their blue eyes were beginning to change to gold. The day finally came when the silver dozen would leave to go live at their furr-ever homes with their new families that they had picked out weeks ago. Well, except Churchill. He picked his family out the day he was born.

He was staying with his mama and sister-chicken, Dolly. He had already been given his cute mustache collar and name tag in case they got lost from him. It was his favorite thing to wear because it was his. His brothers and sisters all bathed, packed with their puppy bags and dressed in their special collars; they waited for the doorbell to ring.

Do YOU have something special that you like to wear?

DING-DONG went the bell.

The puppies were so excited that they darted out the front door to greet their families. Each of the silver puppies bounced into the arms of the very special families they were going home with today.

Mama Bella was so happy
because she knew they
were already so loved.
These not-so-tiny
anymore, furry, squeaky,
silver puppies were
growing up and had
something special to
share with their new
families.
Just like YOU.

What makes YOU
special?

The puppies were all settled into their new families. Clementine was the first puppy born, so she was the oldest. She moved the furthest away because she was going off to college to study to be a veterinarian.

She loves helping other animals, and being a doctor is how she can help them best. Clementine has to study very hard. After class, in her free time, she plays at the park and goes on car rides. She also naps – a whole bunch!

And when she naps, she mostly dreams about the day she will graduate.

What are YOUR dreams?

Aspen lives in the
country on a farm with her
daddy, Max. He is teaching her
to hunt, just like him. He is
an international hunting
guide and travels the world.

When she isn't riding around the farm in the pick-up truck, she is working on her hunting skills and hiding in the thick, tall grass practicing her duck calls. Aspen is very good!

What are YOU good at?

Clancy, known as
Miss Clancy Pants,
went to live with her
boy not too far from
mama Bella. She is
becoming a champion
soccer player. Every night
after dinner, she practices
and practices head shots
and goal blocks,
getting better and better
at soccer.

She got her nickname
because even though
she was the smallest puppy,
she was so spunky.
And she still is!!!

Do YOU have a nickname?

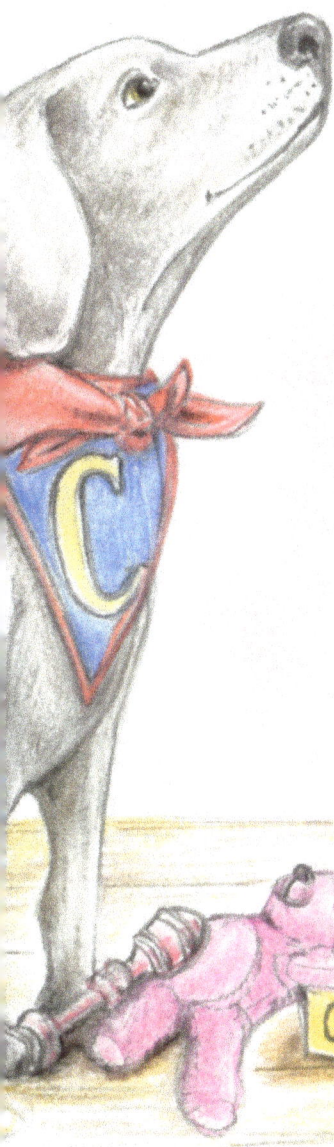

Chance was the first baby in his home, but now has a baby sister who he loves so much. With his long silver legs and courageous instincts, he can leap building blocks in a single bound to protect her. He just loves being her bodyguard. Chance is also so smart. When he is not being Super Dog, he likes to show off tricks he has learned. He is just so clever.

Do YOU know any tricks?

Sterling is a true city princess, but oh does she love the country living. During the week she juggles carpool, workouts (to keep her tiny, silver figure), helping with homework, and multiple schedules for her very busy crew. She is the best 'lil helper.
But the weekends out at her ranch are truly Sterling's "me" time with morning runs around the lake, horseback riding, and swimming and lounging by the pool. She really knows how to relax.

How do YOU relax after a busy week?

Lincoln found his calling early on after leaving
for his new home. He fit into his family right
away. Playtime with his boy and girl is so fun
and tires them all out. They just love their
Lincoln. He ministers unconditional love and
wet kisses to his family all day long, everyday.
But, his night-time ritual is where he truly shines
with his bedtime prayers at tuck-in time.
After storytime, he puts his paws up and his
knees down and gives his thanks and
to them blessings. They all say what they are
thankful for.

Do you have something YOU
are thankful for?

It is no secret Gator lives for his college football games on the weekends (which comes with all the snacks he can forage), hunting trips, and his morning walks before school with his little buddy.

Gator has had to leave for camp and be away from home so that he could train hard to be the best hunter. But, he is most proud that he is, officially, the unofficial mascot to the University of Florida!

Go Gators!

What about YOU makes YOU proud?

Amigo lives down the street from
where he was born and visits with his mom
and Churchill some afternoons when they
are around. Amigo is a masterful,
bilingual, frisbee-catching champion!

He was taught all of his
commands in Spanish only. He wows
the crowd with his athletic skill and
linguistic prowess. He understands
"treat" perfectly in English and
Spanish. Commo se llama?
That is "what is your name?"
in Spanish.

Do YOU know how to speak Spanish?

Isabelle Coco Chanel
(No.5) is a mouthful!
That's why everyone
calls her Izzy.
She was the fifth girl
born, and she was
so ooh-la-la
that no ordinary name
would do. Izzy spends
her days toning the
ladies as a barre instructor
and to stay in shape
herself, but mostly to get
to wear those adorable
workout outfits.
The weekends are
spent cruising on the
water, enjoying the lake
life with her three
favorite boys.

What do YOU enjoy doing
on the weekends?

Blue is the star of his bunch. He
doesn't have a record deal yet, but
he just keeps practicing,
and practicing, and practicing.
When he isn't drumming his tail
to pretty much everything, he is
serenading in his most
convincing, crooning howl, a
tune that will get him the
A-okay to join his family on
the bed for some kisses and
snuggles. It doesn't take much.
Blue is a ROCKSTAR
to his family.
They love his furry snuggles.

Do YOU like to snuggle?

Cooper's number one job was being the best little brother to his boy. They ran and chased the ball until dark and camped out on the couch to watch movies all evening together. He was the brother he always wanted. But then, Cooper decided to do something new. He wanted to go to college. So, he recently moved to live with a new family, and he is now studying to be a lawyer. This was a very brave move. Cooper was scared and nervous at first. He is very happy now.

Do YOU ever get scared or nervous?

After giving his brothers and
sisters a big hug and saying
goodbye, Churchill ran back
into the house and then,
right out the back door. Mama
Bella could hear it before she
could see it. He had done the
biggest belly flop into the pool!
 He yelled out **"yippee"** just as he
hit the water and sent up the biggest
splash! He swam around and around
until his mama told him it was time
for dinner.

Do YOU like to swim?

Churchill loves that he is living at home with mama Bella and his chicken-sister Dolly.

His silver paws perched on the edge of the sofa, he keeps watch out the window. He is very, very good at protecting his family. He barks at EVERYTHING that walks by.

He recently named himself chief security officer, making him in charge of guarding the house…and the front yard, and the neighbors yard.
Well, actually, that is his second job. His first job is being the family's food critic/taster. And honestly, there isn't anything that he's eaten that he hasn't liked.

At first, Churchill had a hard time figuring out what made him special. Then, one day, he realized that just being himself was what made him special.

Everyone is special because YOU are the only YOU.

Every now and then, a sweet boy named
Hudson comes to visit. Churchill gets so
excited to see him because he giggles when he
chases him around. And also because he feeds
him treats. YUM! Playing with Hudson is
very fun! They are friends and will be forever.

Churchill likes to give him very wet kisses,
which also makes him giggle! Hudson loves
to put his arms around Churchill's neck
and give him BIG bear hugs.

Do YOU like to give
BIG bear hugs?

Having birthday parties is so
fun too! Because our mama
thinks we are all so special, we
celebrate our birthday every
year. There are treats, and
balloons, and hats, and
party favors, and singing – very
loud singing. We invite puppy
friends and puppy family
because this is a very,
very, special day.

It is the day the
Silver Dozen
were born!

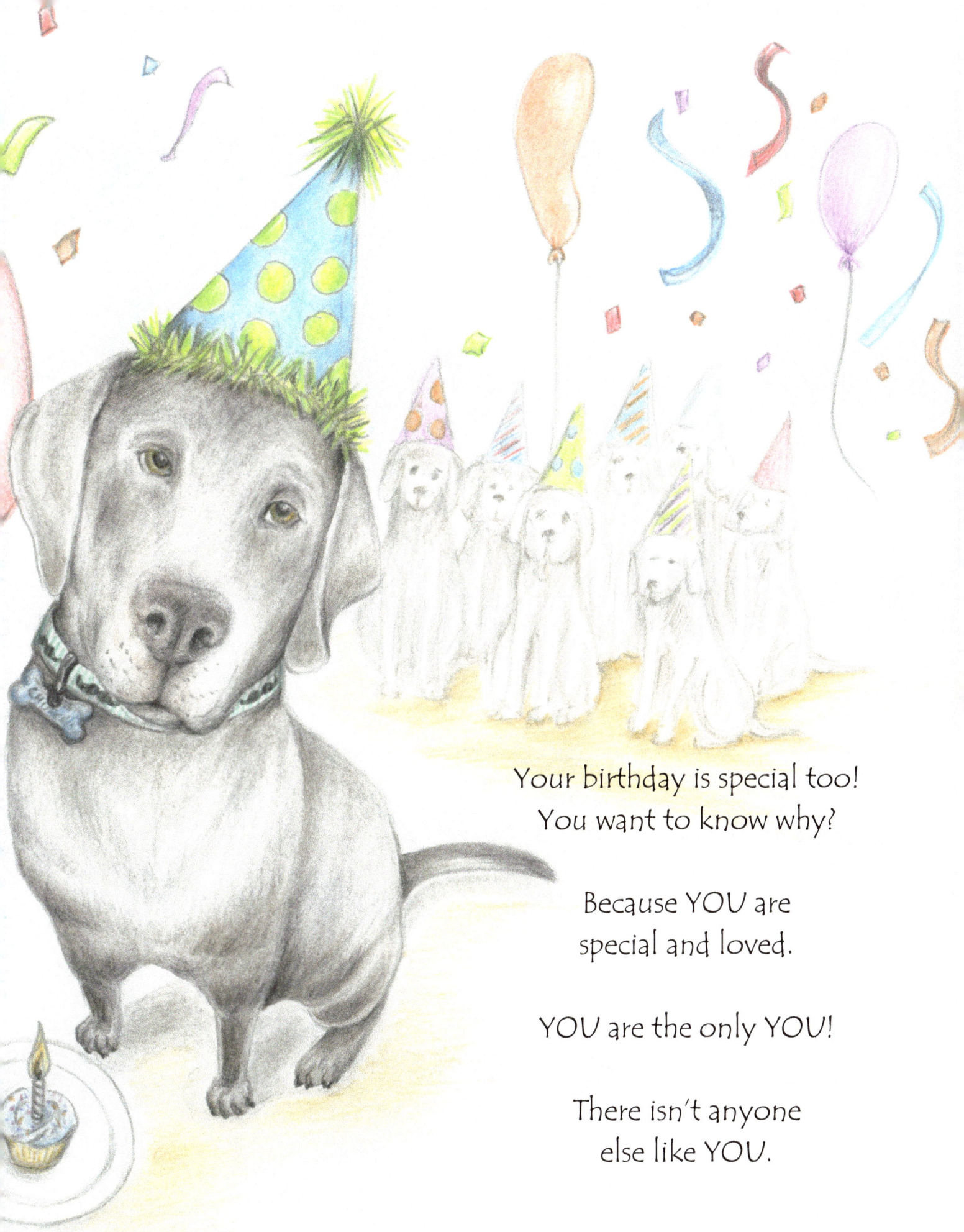

Your birthday is special too!
You want to know why?

Because YOU are
special and loved.

YOU are the only YOU!

There isn't anyone
else like YOU.

This book was inspired by a true story, an unexpected journey of puppy love. Who knew that 12, tiny lil fur- balls could capture my heart and run away with it? I am a confessed softy, and well they are puppies after all. So, probably not hard to imagine. But to me … they are special. I was there when they were born. I even brought to life, the last one born, who made them The Silver Dozen and who is now a part of my family, Churchill. He was mine from that moment forward. They all, however, became my fur babies for the nine weeks that they took over, I mean lived IN my home. It was some of the most treasured three months of my life. Getting up early in my pj's, donning rubber gloves and rain boots to their cheery, sweet, little "squeaky" sounds, to clean their area (12 puppies make some super-cute poopie and pee-pee messes), feed them and take them out to do their business, were some of the most memorable times for me - oh and the puppy piles at night. Watching them pick out their families was heartwarming to witness. Because that's how it happened for most. They walked up to their people and it was a done deal. I am blessed to keep tabs on them all, which nudged me to write this book. As I heard how each was settling in, and making their mark, showing off their talents and specialness in their family, the idea was born. I realized that their journey in a family is to some degree our journey in our own family and life. Given enough time, we all find our gifts, our talents, our specialness. We also learn when necessary, as two families become one, how to blend. Sister-chicken Dolly and Churchill are blending nicely... well most days anyway. And so, although we are all very, very different, even within the same family, we are all special.

We all have a purpose. And, we all matter.

THE GIRLS

IZZY, CLANCY, CLEMENTINE, STERLING, ASPEN

THE BOYS

BLUE, GATOR, AMIGO, LINCOLN, COOPER, CHANCE, CHURCHILL

Marquett Brewster is a mom of three and a Gigi to the first of many, many, many grandbabies. Did I say many? This is her first children's book but probably not her last. Her two silver Labradors and one crazy chicken give her fresh material daily. She lives in Dallas, Texas, where she was born and raised. She loves her friends, family, travel and of course her Tex-Mex food. She is a graduate of Texas Christian University in Fort Worth, Texas. She is also an aspiring novelist.

Anya Studenc Caruso has decades of experience in creative work. She is a graduate of International Fine Arts College, Miami FL. She gives all the credit and praise to the Lord Jesus for these skills. Anya is founder and partner of Engage Inc (engage2connect.com). She dedicates her work in this book to her father, Rudy Studenc, who as an artist himself, first taught her to draw when she was a little girl by outlining horses and other animals in the sand on the beach. He is a great man of creativity, imagination and a believer of following your dreams. She also dedicates her work to her mother, Linda Meyerle, who recognized her daughter's talent early on and always encouraged her to draw/paint by enrolling her in various art classes, buying her drawing/painting supplies and supporting her in attending a college of art.

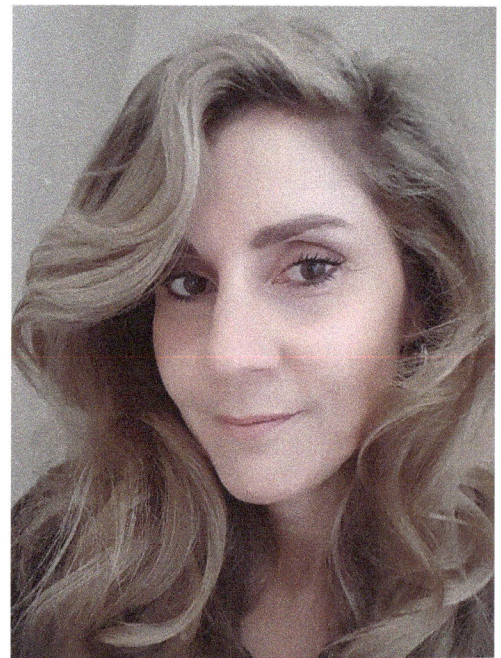

www.ingramcontent.com/pod-product-compliance
Lightning Source LLC
Chambersburg PA
CBHW040317100426
42811CB00012B/1465